contents

In the Garden

There is so much to see in the garden – from beautiful birds that visit for food to pond creatures and **scuttling** reptiles and mammals.

WHAT CAN YOU SEE?

GARDEN

ticktock

Copyright © **ticktock Entertainment Ltd 2006**
First published in Great Britain in 2006 by ticktock Media Ltd.,
Unit 2, Orchard Business Centre, North Farm Road, Tunbridge Wells, Kent TN2 3XF

ISBN 1 86007 854 0
Printed in China

Picture credits
t=top, b=bottom, c=centre, l=left, r=right
Alamy: 4-5. FLPA: 3b, 4-5, 8br, 10-11b, 15b, 19c, 20b, 21t, 23c, 24b.
Every effort has been made to trace the copyright holders, and we apologise in advance for any unintentional omissions.
We would be pleased to insert the appropriate acknowledgements in any subsequent edition of this publication.

A CIP catalogue record for this book is available from the British Library.

What can you see in the garden?

Frog

Water lily

Rabbit

Squirrel

Snail

Sunflower

Honey bee

Mouse

Wren

Frog

The kind of frog that you are most likely to see spends most of its life on land. Its favourite food is insects.

Frogs have long, strong back legs that help them to jump very well.

Frogs lay their eggs in ponds or lakes. Their eggs are called spawn.

Frogs and toads look quite different. Most toads have rough, dry, warty skin.

Toad

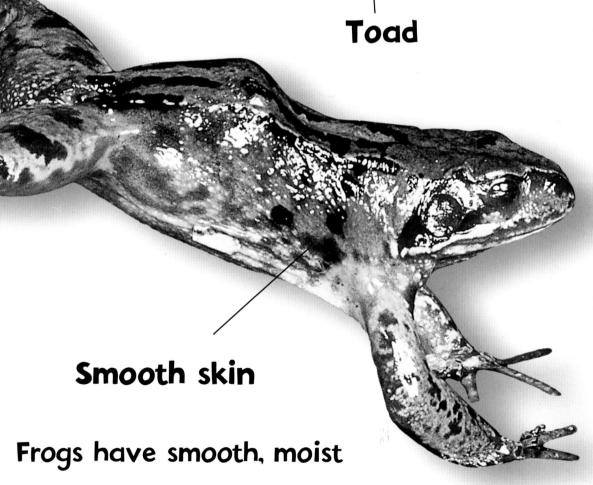

Smooth skin

Frogs have smooth, moist skin. Some frogs feel slimy but others feel dry to the touch.

Water lilies are floating flowers with flat, green heart-shaped leaves. They grow in **freshwater**.

The roots of the water lily grow in the mud at the bottom of a pond or lake.

The plant grows upward until it reaches the surface of the water.

Water lilies appear in a range of beautiful colours, from white and yellow to bright pink.

Rabbit

Rabbits can be seen in meadows and fields, as well as in some gardens.

Rabbits hide in their **burrows** during the day. They come out to eat mostly at night.

When rabbits are not looking after their young, they prefer to be on their own.

Rabbits eat grasses
and plants. They also
eat **crops** like peas,
beans and lettuces.

There are many different kinds of squirrels across the world. Grey squirrels are often seen in gardens.

Squirrels eat nuts, fruit, flowers and plant buds.

Squirrels have learned to steal nuts and seeds from the **feeders** that people put out for birds.

The squirrel's big bushy tail helps it to balance.
It is also used to **communicate** with other squirrels.

 snail

The garden snail has a soft body, **protected** by a hard spiral shell. When the snail is **alarmed**, it tucks itself right inside its shell.

Snails have two pairs of **tentacles** on their heads.

A snail has only one large, flat foot, which **ripples** to move the snail along.

Foot

Snails leave trails of slimy **fluid** called **mucus**.

sunflower

Sunflowers are great fun to grow in the garden. There are many different **varieties.**

Some types of sunflower can grow taller than a person.

Sunflowers have large, bright yellow heads. They turn them to follow the **direction** of the sun.

Female worker bees collect **nectar** from flowers.
This is used to feed the queen bee and bee *larvae*.

MOUSE

Mice are related to rats and there are many different types. If you see one in the garden, it may be a field mouse or harvest mouse.

Mice have grey or brown fur, large ears and a long tail.

Mice can get into houses and cause a lot of damage. They can chew holes in wood.

Harvest or field mice eat seed and grains.

Many different types of birds are known as wrens. Many kinds of wren are quite tiny creatures.

The male wren builds several nests before it looks for a **mate**.

Some wrens nest in holes inside buildings. Others make their homes among plants and trees.

Wrens have a very loud
song call, which is
surprising for such
a small bird.

23

Glossary

Alarmed Scared

Burrow A hole that rabbits and other animals dig to live in

Cell A small separate section or division

Communicate To put across your thoughts to someone else

Crop Plants that are grown for food or other uses

Direction The way in which something is pointing

Drone Name given to a male bee kept in the hive or nest to fertilize eggs laid by the queen bee

Feeder A special container for animal food

Fluid Something that is like water, i.e. not hard

Freshwater Water that isn't salty, i.e. not seawater

Larvae The young of insects

Mate Animal of a different sex

Mucus A slimy covering that coats a living thing to protect it

Nectar Sweet liquid produced by flowering plants

Protect To keep safe from harm

Ripples To move in a wave-like motion

Scuttling To run in a short, hurried way

Tentacle Sensitive growth on an animal's head that is used to feel things

Varieties Different types of the same thing

24